Laughter P

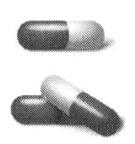

By Angela Johnson Ayers

Copyright (©) 2017 Angela Johnson Ayers

All rights reserved. No part of this book may be reproduced or used in any manner without the express written permission of the author except for the use of brief quotations in a book review.

ISBN 978-1-5441-0556-7

Dedication

I dedicate this book to the only woman I know who encompasses the title, "mommy" in every sense of the word, my mother, Shirley U. Johnson. Is she a perfect person? Of course, not, but was and is she the perfect mother for me, of course so! She sacrificed her dreams, career, time, money and self for her six children. If there is any mother who needed daily capsules of laughter and encouragement to make it through the challenges of motherhood, it is her.

Think about it, six children, a husband, limited finances, transporting us to school, karate, dance, football, soccer, choir, church, camps, etc., etc., etc. On any given day, between the six of us kids, she would drive through two states and the District of Columbia. From Maryland, to DC, to Virginia and back again.

She was like a taxi service and I can honestly say, I NEVER heard her yell or fuss at us for her loaded daily task. I am sure many days went by where she questioned why and how she allowed herself to live such an existence, but if and when she did, we were not the wiser. My fondest memories of my mother were when she was pregnant with my twin brothers. This was a time in her life that was clearly unexpected. I could physically see and feel the stress and frustration she was enduring, but she never gave up and quit.

Despite her pregnancy nausea, and exhaustion, she continued to accompany us on field trips, outings, etc. She may not have always been on time, (smile) but she was always there. Seeing my mom endure that time of her life, and numerous others that created emotional, financial, personal, and physical stress and strain, I ascertained a great deal about female perseverance. We women are awesome and have a God given strength to discern, love and press on.

Mom, if I lived 1000 life times, I could never give you what you have given me. But what I can do is dedicate this book to you for your love, support, dedication, and commitment to your children, your husband and God.

I love, adore and admire you.

Prologue

Do you feel as if your kids are a bit crazy and that they could be driving you even crazier? Do you find yourself stressed and/or worried at times, wondering if you are meeting all you child's mental, emotional, physical, psychological, and spiritual needs? Have your days become monotonous and you need a few minutes of a reprieve?

Whether you are a mom who works away from home, or a stay home mom like myself, one thing we all have in common is the need to laugh and find humor and joy amongst the daily demands, pressures and concerns of motherhood. Being a mom has not been an easy feat for me. I became a first-time mother at the age of 38 and birthed our second child at 42. The adjustment of having lives depend on me 24/7 was, and at times, still is a serious undertaking.

To prevent me from morphing into a yelling, screaming, mommy banshee, I've learned to find humor in everyday situations and events. Before I became a mom, I never knew words like *poop, boogers, mucus,* and *butt cheeks* could send children into a hysterical downward spiral, all while thinking, "I wish they would shut the heck up!" Some say that laughter is the best medicine, and if that is true, we moms need a daily overdose of hard core, lethal prescription medicine administered through a vein drip! Until such a medical, legal laughter antidote is created, this book must suffice.

I wrote this book because we moms are in a sisterhood and have more in common than differences. I am sure a great number of things mentioned in this book have happened to you, your children, your life, making it even funnier knowing you are not alone. I provide a 31-day supply of "Laughter Prescriptions Pills," and "Encouragement Pills" for you to read; or keeping with the medicine theme, take daily.

In the event you are having a rough day and need a double dose of giggles, or a word of encouragement, go ahead and read, I mean, ingest all the pills in one sitting. Just pop open the book (bottle), take at least one capsule by mouth daily, laugh and enjoy!

Love and much laughter,

Angela

Day 1 Laughter Capsule
"Dear God, Please Help Mom Outgrow Her Fat!!!"

Yes, you read that right. That was a heartfelt and serious prayer that my 4-year-old daughter prayed during our night time family devotion. Let me tell you how it all went down. After Larry and I read a passage in the Bible, we let the girls say their individual prayers, followed by kisses, hugs and off to sleepy land they go (most of the time it goes this smooth). Well, this one night, the evening routine was going great.

They had both used the bathroom, drank water and were in bed. I said, "Ok, who wants to pray first?"
Our 8-year-old says, "I do" and she went on to thank God for the day we had and to ask God to bless others who did not have much in life. Oh, how proud I was to hear her pray for others. I had a grin on my face that read, "Boy, I don't totally suck at this mommy thing after all. Surely God must have great favor towards me by allowing my kids to be so selfless."

Well, next I say, "OK Lilly, it is your turn to pray!" Now mind you, I was still relishing in my spiritual epiphany of what an awesome mom God must think I am, when I hear the 4-year-old say, "Dear God, PLEASE HELP MOM OUTGROW HER FAT, AMEN!" In my mind, I said, "What the hell!" Yes, I am ashamed to admit that in mid prayer, this unholy phrase came to my mind with a thrust like a rushing wind. Nothing Godly or spiritual about that.

When I looked in Lilly's face, I could tell she was serious as a heart attack and was truly praying to God about a matter that she felt warranted divine intervention. I also could not believe how loud Aunna, was laughing in her bedroom. Matter of fact, Aunna found Lilly's prayer so hysterical, till she came running into Lilly's room, where I was standing, to make sure she heard Lilly correctly.

Aunna and I both said at the same time, "Lilly what did you pray?" And without skipping a beat, my precious, loving, caring, God fearing 4-year-old says, "I said, God please help mommy outgrow her fat!" As soon as she finished repeating the word fat, Aunna fell to the floor laughing as if Richard Prior, Dave Chapelle, Gabriel Iglesias, Kevin Hart, and Eddie Murphy were all doing stand-up routines at the same time in front of us.

She was laughing so hard and loud till I had to tell her to "shut up" and go to her room. All the while, Lilly is looking like, "what is so funny?" Obviously, I had to laugh too because of the sincerity and faith she had in God. Lastly, I was taken aback because I pride myself for coming a LONGGGGG way when it comes to my weight.

In 2006 I was at my heaviest weight of 318 lbs. As of today, I have lost over 140 lbs. So, knowing all this background info., you can see why I was taken for a loop by this heart felt petition my 4-year-old made to God. Now grant it, my arms and stomach are a bit "floppy" as the kids tell me, but MY GOODNESS, "outgrow my fat!" INDEED!

But you know what? I graciously thanked Lillian for her earnest prayer and rather than let it worry me and make me subconscious about my weight, I found a "silver lining." Despite all my "mommy shortcomings," knowing that Larry and I have instilled in the children Godly values and the power of prayer, that's what matters most. And to assist God in helping me "outgrow my fat," I make sure I work a little bit harder at the gym.

Day 2 Laughter Capsule
You Are Probably a Mom if You……

1. If you have ever uttered the words, "Sit down and Shut Your Mouth!" you are probably a mom.

2. If you have ever been driving and then had to reach one arm around your seat to slap or hit someone on the leg or in the mouth, you are probably a mom.

3. If you have ever waited till late at night to eat your favorite treat in peace and quiet without having to share with a single soul, you are probably a mom.

4. If you have ever sat out front of your home in the car, using it as a makeshift retreat where you can be alone to think, listen to music, cry, scream, meditate, eat, drink, and/or sleep, you are probably a mom.

5. If you have ever been in a store, hear a baby crying, and able to discern if the cry is due to

hunger, sleepiness, pain, or needing to be changed, you are probably a mom.

6. If you have been in the checkout line at a store and the lady behind you is trying to calm down a tantrum throwing toddler, and you do not judge her, you are probably a mom.

7. If you hide extra non-perishable food and drink items in the trunk of your vehicle so it won't get eaten up in one day, you are probably a mom.

8. If you know the names of all the restaurants where children eat free with an adult purchase, you are probably a mom.

9. If you have memorized the entire lineup of shows on Disney, Disney Jr., Nick, Nick Jr., Cartoon Network, Discovery Family, Sprout, and the Hallmark channel, you are probably a mom.

10. If you find yourself reminiscing about all the good sleep you got when you were single, you are probably a mom.

Day 3 Laughter Capsule
Where Are All the Forks and Spoons?

I am convinced there is an invisible elf that magically appears in my kitchen during the night while we are fast asleep, whose sole purpose is to steal my cutlery. It seems as if every morning I wake, there is one less fork or spoon in the house. I have no clue how they keep disappearing, and when I ask the children and hubby, they look at me as if I have two heads, three ears and twelve lips. No one ever knows how our forks and spoons keep vanishing. I am ready to set up some high tech, military style, heat activated surveillance cameras just to pinpoint the culprit.

I mean really! Forks and spoons do not just walk away, but maybe they do. Maybe the silverware is pissed off at the brand dish washing detergent I am using and just can't take it anymore. Or perhaps my food is not up to their liking…….NO, I know that isn't it! I got it! Maybe, just maybe, these disappearing forks and spoons are sick of my children using them as drum sticks, swords and lollipops, therefore they have absconded to a faraway land never to be found again.

Whatever the reason, and wherever they are, I have one simple request. The next time they plan to run away, and I know there will be a next time, simply take some knives along for the journey. I have an abundance of knives that are extremely lonely in the cutlery drawer now that their more popular counterparts have vanished, and the last thing I need is for the children to find a use for the knives.

Day 4 Laughter Capsule
"Really Dude? You Don't Know How to Clean the Tub/Shower!"

I am convinced that husbands lie about not being able to clean the bathtub/shower as good as we women can. I pride myself on keeping a clean and tidy home. The two areas that I am totally anal retentive about, with a touch of OCD are the bathrooms and kitchen. I clean the tubs and showers after the children and I bath times. So, whenever my dear, sweet, attentive husband takes a shower, I make sure the cleaning detergent and sponge is strategically placed next to the tub so he has no excuse for not cleaning upon shower completion.

But it never ceases to amaze me that he seems incapable of cleaning the tub/shower adequately. I truly think this guy has selective blindness when it comes to scrubbing the tub. He does not need x-ray vision to see the soap scum ring that is present after he "cleans" it. Matter of fact, I am convinced that Larry has selective blindness and paralyzes, because I have seen him wash and detail his vehicle as if the life of our children and future grandchildren depends on it!

Come on ladies, think about it! Every Saturday morning, husbands across this fine country find the strength and fortitude to fill up a bucket with the best of car washing solutions, mix it with warm water, lather up and clean their vehicles. Not only do they lather up the vehicles from top to bottom, but they have created their own specific style of moving the wash rag/sponge from one side to the other without a single smear or smudge. They have perfected their "brush strokes" to the point where it should become an Olympic sport.

I find myself gazing out the window wondering, "how is it that this man can scrub an entire vehicle from roof to wheels, thus removing any and every ounce of dirt and grime, however, he cannot seem to master the art of cleaning a bathtub/shower?" Ladies it is quite simple. Husbands suffer from a long and tragic sickness called **TUBSCRUBBINGNESIA**!

This non-life threatening condition causes a man to selectively forget how to scrub and or clean a specific item or room inside your home. If you are unsure that your man suffers from this, let me help you diagnose with a list of symptoms:

- Lying when you ask if they washed the tub/shower after use.
- Wetting the sponge/clothe that you have set aside for cleaning in hopes that you will see that the rag is wet and assume they cleaned the tub.
- He tells you, "the lighting in the bathroom is too dim for me to see the ring around the tub."
- Saying that the cleaning solution is not heavy duty enough and that is why it appears that the area is still dirty.
- "I just am not as good a cleaner as you are honey!"
- "You clean it this time and show me again how you want it done!"

Now these are just a few of the many symptoms husbands may display. If that is your case, please DO NOT panic. This is totally normal for this ailment. I am sure a cure does exist or will one day. I just am not aware when and how the antidote will be made available.

So, ladies, you may be asking yourselves, "what am I to do while waiting for this medication to be created and or discovered?" Great question! The answer is simply this, accept the fact that your husband is incapable of cleaning the tub/shower to your standards. Thank him for the effort he makes when he does clean it and then guilt him into taking you out for ice cream in his sparkling, dazzling clean, spotless, soap scum free vehicle that he mustered the strength and insight to wash.

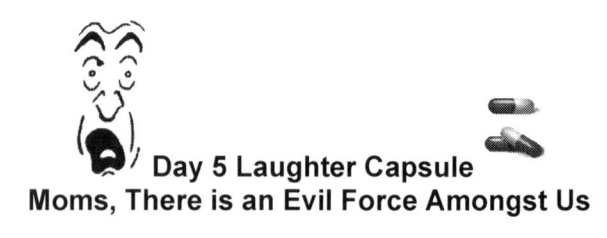

Day 5 Laughter Capsule
Moms, There is an Evil Force Amongst Us

My fellow moms, there is a force living, breathing and growing amongst us that is more powerful than you and I combined. Only a few fortunate souls have been able to destroy the impact of it. This power draws parents in through the insistence of our children needing and wanting it. It is pretty, quite gorgeous with its sparkled appearance and free falling ability to beautify everything and everyone it encapsulates. Children of all ages, and races use it for crafts, homework assignments, etc.

This force that I speak of can be found in all craft stores 365 days a year, 366 in a leap year. Please beware, because once you open this mighty item, it NEVER leaves. This substance I speak of is G L I T T E R! Yes, arts and craft glitter is the enemy ladies.

I curse the days whenever my kids say, "Mom, we need glitter for crafts!" No matter how well you clean up after using glitter, it's never all gone. Like a houseguest from hell, although they may physically leave your home, their residue last for weeks. The same is true for glitter.

Water, soap, bleach, disinfectant cleanser, sponges, paper towels, napkins, you name it, I have tried it all to clean up after a glitter session. And to no avail, it's residue stays. Heck, the glue my kids use to sprinkle the glitter on top of cleans up better than the glitter itself. I am still finding patches of glitter on my floor from the Christmas decoration crafts we created months ago. And let's not mention the glitter that makes its way on every part of your body.

The other day while getting dressed, I noticed my left leg was sparking. As I studied the situation a bit further, I spotted a conglomeration of purples, reds, silvers and golds twinkling simultaneously, and it hit me, Glitter! It took me 10 minutes, rubbing alcohol and a rhythmic circular motion to rid my body of it.

My daughters love to visit craft stores on a weekly basis to stock up on supplies. When we walk close to the glitter aisle, I feel myself beginning to hyperventilate and pray to God above that they do not have glitter on their list. At times, I have found myself lying to the children saying that the store was out of glitter.

Of course, they saw past my façade and gently instructed me to turn around and look on the shelf to the left. As I slowly turned, there it was, my arch enemy, glaring back at me as if Mr. Glitter knew I hated his very existence. As the girls grabbed two huge containers, which just happened to be on sale for buy one, get one free, I began an unholy tirade of mental profanity that would make a sailor blush.

Moms, I am not sure what we can do to rid our lives of this nuisance. Protesting and boycotting will not help because glitter is a desired and needed evil for our offspring. It can beautify any and everything it touches. It makes holidays pretty and special, and can assist in getting your child an A+ on a school project. So, we must come to the realization that glitter is and will be a part of our lives, at least until our children go to college.

In the meantime, I am throwing up the white flag of surrender and taking the girls to the hobby store this weekend to purchase more glitter. I have a 20 % off coupon. Heck, if you can't beat them, join them.

Day 6 Laughter Capsule
Teenagers are From Out of Space and Have Super Powers

When you think of characters with super powers, Superman, Wonder Woman, Batman, Captain America, etc. may come to mind., along with their costumes and specific enemy fighting abilities. Superman could fly, run fast, and had x-ray vision to name a few. Wonder Woman used her bracelets and belt, along with other tools to bring down "bad guys." I am here to tell you about a specific group of individuals that also obtain super powers beyond yours and mines comprehension. These human entities are between the ages of 13-19, usually wear clothing that range from cool to totally insane and are social media experts. The name that these beings go by is TEENAGERS! Teenagers are from another planet and have super powers that little kids and adults do not possess.

Seriously! Now you are probably asking, "Well Angela, what are these super powers you speak of?" I will tell you, thanks for asking. One power is called the ability to lie through their teeth without breaking a sweat. Think about it. Ask your teen who ate the last piece of cake and observe their response. Or, inquire as to whether they completed their homework and wait to be amazed at the lying superpower that will spew out of their mouths. This ability can manifest itself in a verbal response, physical movement/gesture or grunt, but unbeknownst to them, we adults can see through their smoke and mirror performance.

The second super power is found on the bottom of their feet. They can literally spot an object on the floor, and rather than pick it up, walk directly on top of it without any pain or discomfort. Their aptitude to tread on top of any material or substance, hard or soft, that could potentially cripple us mere mortals, never ceases to amaze me. Just observe a teen in their natural habitat, their bedroom. Stand at the doorway quietly and peer into the room. Do not walk in for fear of stepping onto something that could potentially permanently damage your mortal feet. Take close and careful notes when witnessing them walk from point A to point B in search of an item all while trampling over pens, pencils, paper, shoes, books, candy bar wrappings, balls, etc. As they tread, not one time will they flinch or bend down to remove the item. Amazing!

The third super power these weird creatures possess is their aptitude to text at speeds quicker than light travels. If the International Olympic Committee is in search of a new, competitive sport, teenage texting would be a must-see event. Now I know what you are thinking. You are wondering if these aliens will ever morph into mortals.

The answer is, YES, probably around the age of 20. Just like in any group, there are a few anomalies that defy the odds and throw a monkey wrench into the most profound and in-depth scientific and experimental hypothesis. Thankfully, I have run across a few of these teen relics. You must search far and wide for them, but if you are fortunate, and the stars, moon and planets all align, you will spot a "normal," "non-alien" teen one day.

Day 7 Laughter Capsule
"I Think I Pushed Out My "Sex Mojo" When I Gave Birth to My Children, & I'm Determined to Get It Back!"

Fellow moms, when I was younger and without children, I was on FIRE! No one told me that after having children, my sex drive would change. I was totally not prepared for it. I realize there are various factors that contribute to a mother's low libido, like exhaustion, sleep deprivation, hormones, anxiety, stress, age, etc., but I was certainly taken off guard. I just figured that after my 6-week vaginal healing from child birth, my mojo would be up and popping.

So, when that did not happen, I was on a quest to find it and get it back! Ladies, let me tell you just how desperate I was to reunite with my inner sex kitten. I went to this lady who is an herbalist. I call her a "good witch doctor" because her store is located miles from civilization and from the outside it looks like a scary, old log cabin/old time county store found only in horror movies. I did not let the appearance frighten me off though. I was on a mission, "Operation Get My Mojo Back."

As I entered this horror film cliché store, my nose was bombarded with a barrage of herbal smells. As far as the eye could see, there was nothing but jars, on top of jars of teas, herbs, pills, soaps, oils, etc., all claiming to be natural, with healing properties. As I explained to one of the workers what my dilemma was, she insisted that I speak to the owner and chief herbalist.

Suddenly, a short, plain faced, white haired woman emerges. Taken aback by her homely appearance, but desperate all the same, I explained that I needed something to boost libido. She assumed that it was for my husband. I told her emphatically, "NO, it's for me! She smiled and began spewing out herbal terms that flew over my head like a 747 jet.

After suggesting various "remedies," I asked the dreaded question; "how much will all this cost?" Once I heard the cost to purchase my sex mojo, I explained that I was desperate, but on a budget. Again, she observed me with a strange, almost scary smirk and handed me a reasonably priced self-steeping tea. I quickly paid and got out of there before night fall, and the "boogeyman" could catch me.

Now mind you, just that morning, I told my husband where I was going and that hopefully I would be returning with a tea I could drink to help me, help him (wink, wink). Well, I swear he must have started boiling water time I called to inform him I was on my way home, because when I walked into the house, I would bet my life that I heard our tea kettle whistling.

I looked at him, called him an idiot under my breath like I usually do, trotted to the kitchen, then anxiously grabbed my steeper and a mug. I poured the piping hot water over the tea and drank, drank, drank. After every cup, Larry would glare into my eyes as if my mojo would telepathically inform him that my body was ready for AMORE (love).

I do not think the tea helped that much. Maybe it was mental, but, as long as I was guzzling the beverage, I could muster up a little extra energy to perform my "wifely duties" a tad bit more, but I was not at 100 percent. Ladies, I am not sure if I will ever be like I was years ago.

Other women have told me that as the kids get older and require less of my physical energy, my mojo will return.

Until it returns full force, I will keep on exercising, destressing my life and simply embracing the love and attraction my dear husband has for me. There is an old saying that states, "practice makes perfect." I am hoping that the more I "practice," the more I want to practice (smile.)

Day 8 Laughter Capsule
Mom, I'm Sorry I Called You STUPID Behind Your Back!!!

I guess my youngest child could not stand the guilt of her actions, so one fine morning, she walks into our bedroom and says, "Mom, I'm sorry I called you stupid!" I said, "When did you call me stupid, baby?" I am sure I would have remembered that, even if my "brain is broken," as my kids tell me when I cannot remember something they told me a week earlier.

She proceeded to confess and sing like a canary and say, "I said it yesterday behind your back after you told me I could not have an Oreo cookie." I did not know whether to laugh and smile for the innocent candor that she was displaying, or ask her what other horrible things she uttered or thought about me once I turned my back to leave a room. Instead, I thanked her for her honesty and gave her two Oreo cookies!

Day 9 Encouragement Capsule
"My Boobs, National Geographic or Playboy Magazine?"

When I was a little girl, my parents subscribed to National Geographic Magazine. It was filled with colorful, in depth photos and articles about people, places, customs, artifacts, etc. from various parts of the world. This magazine transported me to faraway lands and greatly informed me on topics not always covered in classrooms. National Geographic Magazine existed way before the internet did. Each page that I turned, was, in a way, my own pre-internet search engine.

Asia, Africa, Australia, the Rain Forest, mountains, caves, etc., each article gave me insight and knowledge. My favorite National Geographic Magazine issues was when I was around 10 years old and it focused on a few countries in Africa. No stone was left unturned. Gorgeous, colorful images of the people, clothing, food, land, sunsets, animals, buildings, safari, you name it, it was covered. But one interesting image stood out, the physical appearance of a few of the women.

These ladies were beautiful and it was apparent that their dark, smooth, silky skin had been kissed long by the radiant African sun. After being mesmerized by their beauty, my 10-year-old self could not help but notice that they were naked from the waist up. Their breast hung low down in a way that I just assumed came from not wearing bras, as well as breast feeding their young far longer than mommies did in richer Continents and countries. I chalked it up to that and never questioned it again. To me, it simply added to their cultural and ethnic beauty and regality.

Let's fast-forward to the present. I find myself staring into the bathroom mirror upon entering and exiting the shower, and am amazed at how my once full, ample breast, now resemble the attractive African women I learned about 35 years prior. The other day I was standing naked (with the door closed & locked to prevent nosey kids from barging in), looking in the mirror holding my breast up, then down, up then down.

I called Larry to the room. He knocks, I unlock the door, and lock and close quickly. When he notices that I am naked, he gets a stupid grin on his face and proceeds to undress faster than a speeding bullet. I swiftly say, "DUDE, no, not going down right now. I want to show you something!"

As he begins to put his clothes back on, I say, "Look Larry, National Geographic Breast." Then I take my hands and pull my breast up as if I had gotten an instant breast lift and say, "Now, Playboy Magazine Breast." I then go back and forth holding my breast up, then letting them hang low, holding them up and then letting them hang low, all while quoting, "National Geographic Breast, Playboy Breast, National Geographic Breast, Playboy Breast!"

At this junction, Larry is very confused, yet slightly turned on, but when he observes the serious look on my face, he poses a question like only he can. He states, "Angela, what the hell is wrong with you?" I chuckle a bit and then tell him how I wish my breast looked perkier like the young 25-year old's in Playboy, rather than them hanging low like I was still breast feeding.

I tell him about the African ladies and described to him how their breast appeared. In true Larry fashion, he says, "Angela, first, how many Playboy magazines have you viewed?" I say, "not many." He then states, "Angela, half those women in there probably had some work done and secondly, didn't you once tell me that you found those African women in National Geographic stunning, strong and regal?" Again, I say, "Yes."

He then verbalizes something that blew me away. He responds, "Angela, what made those African women beautiful is their breast told a story. Their low hanging breast symbolized strength, dignity, nurturing and life. They use their breast to provide and sustain life. Also, they know and understand that their identity, beauty, and self-worth had nothing to do with the fullness, size and/or volume of their breast. They were not their breast!" Then he kissed me on my forehead and left out the room.

As I began to get dressed, my mind replayed repeatedly all what Larry had spoken. He was so right. A woman's breast reveals a story, regardless of the size, shape, color, or volume. Some breasts communicate the story of surviving breast cancer, a mastectomy, pregnancy/child birth, or leaving an abusive relationship. A great number of female's breast tells the story of overcoming obstacles, stereotypes, poverty and low self-esteem.

Yours may translate the story of finally taking control of your health and appearance by losing weight and treating yourself to breast augmentation surgery to accentuate your true beauty. You see, my breast symbolizes strength, hope, dreams, courage, love, pain, fear, victory and triumph. Whatever the reason, instead of shaking my head in disgust at my breast, I allow them to portray my life story as being a strong, determined woman who has overcome a bad first marriage, miscarriage, obesity and low self-esteem.

Would I still like to have my breast touched up if I had the money? Yes, in a way, and no in another. Part of me loves the fact that my sagging breast came at a cost. The cost and blessing of birthing children and getting older. The other half of me, the vain side, wants to see a pair of ample breast looking perky and perfect. But until then, I will wear these God given breast with dignity and pride just like those amazing, elegant, regal African women did 35 years ago.

Day 10 Laughter Capsule
"Sit Down, Shut Up and Eat Your Da#* Food!"

I have been cooking food since I was 10 years old. Being the second oldest of six children, you learn quick, fast and in a hurry how to assist in making your moms life a bit easier. So, for as long as I can remember, being in the kitchen, cooking and preparing meals is like second nature to me. I pride myself on my cooking abilities.

Shoot, you name it, I can cook it. Southern style, Italian, Vegetarian, Asian, etc. Breakfast, lunch, dinner and snacks I can prepare effectively and efficiently. So, it really burns me up and sends me to a very dark, dark place, when I work hard preparing meals and these children say things like; "I don't want this!" "Mom, this looks gross!" "Why did you fix this?"

Well, my response to them has been, "What I want you all to do is Sit Down, Shut Up and Eat Your Da#& Food!" Listen, I know it is not good nor Godly to use "choice" words towards and around kids. But haven't your children pissed you off so bad complaining and fussing, till the only words that bring you relief and satisfaction are the ones that you should not say to them?

Okay, maybe it is just me and maybe I need to pray harder and read my Bible more often, but to be honest with you, I have no shame or regret telling my little complainers to eat their dam% food! Should I feel bad? I am told that I should, but darn it, I work HARD! Very Hard.

I cook, clean, sew, transport them to activities, school, doctor appointments. I pay bills, set up bill arrangements, I do laundry, iron clothes, vacuum, grocery shop, hair, etc. etc. etc. Therefore, the least they can do is appreciate a good meal and eat it without complaining.

When I was a child, I NEVER fussed about a meal. Maybe it was because I was chubby, loved food and never saw a meal I did not like. Having "picky" kids of my own makes me feel deep down inside as if I have failed in some way as a mom. Ok, I am about to get really deep and put my Counseling hat on.

As moms, when our children rebel against something we say, make, or do, in some ways it psychologically and emotionally makes one, think that if we were better parents, they would not rebel. But the truth is, our children have their own minds and opinions, and this is a good thing.

As parents, it is our job to guide them in the proper, most impactful way for them to exist, behave, communicate, eat, live, etc. It is not a failure on our part when they assert their will and desires. They are simply using, or in some cases, not using their free-will properly.

Although I know this, it still hurts and frustrates me when they do not eat what I prepare. To cut down on my frustration level, as well as preventing meal time from becoming a "crazy mom bonanza," I simply make the meals. If they eat, fine, and if they don't, cereal it is! It's not worth raising my blood pressure nor using words that will probably send me sprinting to the alter at Sunday worship service seeking repentance.

Day 11 Laughter Capsule
Pasta Down the Drain

I hate to waste anything. Time, words, money, food, etc., you name it, I can't stand to waste it. So, you can imagine how upset at myself I get whenever I try to strain pasta without using a strainer and most of it goes bounding down the drain. You may be wondering, how someone like myself, a "waste hater," finds herself being too lazy to pull out the strainer and use it. Well, that is a great question, and the answer is, my ego!

I like to think that I am such a precise and amazing cook, till I do not need some "stupid" strainer to pour off water. I mean really, how hard could it be to partially cover a pot with its lid and empty the water, all while maintaining perfect al dente pasta? I guess in my case, it is a bit of a challenge, and maybe I should strongly consider either taking a "pasta draining" course at the local community college, or stop being prideful and lazy and keep the strainer on the counter near the sink as I cook.

That way, I do not have to waste money taking a class, nor waste flawless, taste arousing pasta down my sinks drain. I cannot promise that I will never attempt to succeed in my quest to strain pasta sans a strainer, but what I can promise is a great meal, with or without pasta!

Day 12 Laughter Capsule
"Mom, What is BEAROPAUSE?"

I had just picked Aunna up from school and we were cruising along in the car. Everything was going great. No one was hitting or kicking the other. Lilly was almost asleep, and fighting it like only she can, and Aunna was gazing out the window……when suddenly she asked, "Mom, didn't you say that menopause was when a woman is 50 and stops getting her period?" I smile and say, "Well, all things considered, that is almost accurate. Some women stop getting their periods earlier than age 50, some later. Menopause differs from woman to woman, but you are right, menopause is the end of a female's menstrual cycle."

She then explains that her friend at school's mom is 50 and just gave birth to another child. We discussed how a great number of females have babies after age fifty, but that she will not have to ever worry about me following in their footsteps. I hadn't finished my sentence good when Lilly, the 4-year-old "comes to life" and ask, "Mom, what is BEAROPAUSE?" I hesitated and said, "WHAT?" At this point, Lilly is annoyed because not only am I not understanding what she is asking, but her sister is cracking up laughing at her inquiry.

Lilly repeats her question, and this time, louder and with more force. "I SAID, what is BEAROPAUSE? You were talking to Aunna about Bearopause!" Ladies, I had to laugh, but quickly compose myself before she went into meltdown mode and commenced to calling her sister names.

I said, "Lilly, I was talking to your sister about menopause, a time a female no longer gets her menstrual period. It is pronounced men o pause, not bear o pause." Instantly she calms down and all is right with the world, at least till we get home and they have another sister to sister verbal sparring session.

So, moms, if you or anyone you know is suffering from any of the side effects that menopause encompasses, feel comforted to know you are not alone, per my four-year-old, bears also suffer from menopause.

Day 13 Laughter Capsule
The Key to Being a Great Mom to Young Children...... LIE to THEM!

Yes, you read it right! I LIE to my children. I must for my sanity and the sanity of my household. Now let's be honest with one another, children cannot handle too much truth. Kids today want to know everything, all the time. I am one of those parents who takes the time to explain answers to my kid's questions because I do not want them to be ignorant, but come on! Sometimes you need to lie to them just to shut them up and keep it moving.

For example, if I hear, "Mom, this taste funny, did you put sugar in it like I want?" My response, "Yes dear I did" (knowing full well I did not). Or, "Mom, can we go to Chuck E Cheese today?" My response, "No baby, it is closed today for annual cleaning!" Or, "Mommy, did you remember to DVR Sesame Street?" My response, "Dear, the cable company was working on the satellite today, so I was unable to record (knowing full well I forgot)."

I am not advocating for making lying a normal part of your relationship. I am just letting you know that I understand when and why some of you do "stretch the truth" from time to time.

I'm aware that children must be told no, wait, not now, as well as hear unpleasant truths, but there are just some times when you must pick and choose your battles. I am not a medical doctor or mental health provider, so I am in no wise offering professional advice. I am simply a mom who weighs my options and must discern if my nerves can handle a kid melt down if the truth is exposed.

You are probably wondering if I plan to continue to lie to my children when they get older. My response is simply; I will stop lying to them when pigs start flying, and if I'm lying, I'm flying!

Day 14 Laughter Capsule
"Mom, What Did They Call Trucks in the Old Days When You Were a Kid"?

Reality hits hard when your child refers to your childhood as "the old days!" While driving in the car transporting kids from point A to point B, my mind was off in La La land when from the back seat of the car I hear, "MOM, did they have trucks in the OLD DAYS when you were a kid?!" This question caught me off guard to the point where I did not answer. I had to come out of my thoughts and ask myself, how old does this kid think I am? "Old Days?" "What the heck!?"

Then the reality hit me, my kids think about my youth like I use to think of my parent's younger years. When my parents, especially my dad, would "enlighten" my siblings and I on his upbringing and all that it encompassed, my mind would paint pictures of him walking miles to and from school, with holes in his shoes and clothes that were worn and tattered. To be honest, in my youthful mind, I visualized my dad's childhood like a scene from Little House on the Prairie.

Now mind you, today my parents are in their 70's, thus placing my dad's birth year around the 1940's, but the images of Prairie life and horse and buggy I dreamed of were a bit outdated. The same out dated images my daughters have about my younger years, are now being painted with the same "outdated" brush I use to paint my parent's childhood with.

As I was getting ready to answer her inquiry, I could not help but wonder if this line of questioning was created by me, their mom. Think about it, most generation of parents seem to refer to their "childhood" in ways that seemed a bit antiquated, simpler, yet harder, and more taxing than their present world. Maybe, instead of looking at my kid crossed eyed when this question blindsided me, perhaps it was my fault.

What if the stories I tell my children about my youth sound like times of old; really old? Perhaps we parent's, from the beginning of time, have been painting a less than favorable picture of our lives "BC" (before children)? Can you imagine the stories Adam and Eve must have told Caine and Abel in regards to "the good old days" in the garden of Eden? WOW!

There is an old saying I have heard my mom recite from time to time; "Every generation is weaker, but wiser!" Maybe there is some truth to that! With every new generation; technology, science, and medicine, to name a few categories, seem to open and expand knowledge and insight, thus making each generation wiser. However, in my opinion, with new and savvier technology, there are drawbacks that can make one mentally, physically, and socially weaker.

Think about it! Most young people today do not know how to form meaningful, personal relationships because they think having the most "likes," "friends," and "followers" on social media constitutes relationships. And let's not get started on the way technology has eliminated the need for patience because everything from food to information is instant. No one writes letters, or calls or even visits anymore. Heck, just press a button and you get darn near anything and everything you want, need and dream of.

So, to prevent my kids from connecting my younger days to the horse and buggy, pre-vehicle decade, I will clean my "image creating paint brush" and create a canvas full of exact and specific depictions. And if that does not help, I will just shake my head in disbelief, smile and tell them to take out their electronic devices and Google the words, "life in 1971!"

Day 15 Laughter Capsule
"Mom, Ask Google, She Knows EVERYTHING!"

Since you and I were just talking about technology, I thought this story would give you a chuckle. The other day, driving in the car, OF COURSE, the kids start tossing questions at me as if I was playing the lightening round on Jeopardy. Questions about life, art, vegetation, etc. You name it, for some insane reason, they think I am a certified genius who holds all of life's answers in my bosom. I rolled my eyes up in my head as far as they could physically travel, gripped the stirring wheel tighter and said in my "I am sick of these kid's voice," WHAT CHILD?

Next I hear, "Mom, how many trees are in the world?" When I did not respond quick enough, they began tossing out numbers that ranged from the ridiculous to the absurd! Shoot, they were making up numbers that would cause a mathematician to contemplate a career change. Abruptly one of the little critters yells out, "MOM, don't worry, just ask Google, SHE KNOWS EVERYTHING!"

Instantly my mind traveled back to how I use to find information. Encyclopedias were my search engines. I loved the smell of encyclopedias and how the pages were filled with facts, photos and countless data that kept me in a perpetual state of academic excitement. With every page, I found joy and elation in the hunt. The more I had to seek out the information, the more accomplished and scholarly I felt.

Dictionaries and thesauruses, dinosaurs of our past, were in almost every room in our home growing up. I recall utilizing them often to look up the spelling and definition of words I was not sure of. And let's not mention the tedious process of performing research in college. Waiting my turn in line to use the microfiche machine, spending hours reading and copying information and then trucking to the computer lab to type up my papers since laptops and personal PC's were too expensive for most to afford at the time.

During my drive down memory lane, my thoughts were interrupted by, "Mom did you hear what we said, ask Google?" I giggled and proceeded to explain how daunting a process it use to be to gather information, and how blessed they are to live in a time when by a touch or swipe, instant knowledge. I also found myself feeling sorry for them. Has all this technology made young people of today lazy and entitled?

Knowing that they do not have to put forth much physical and mental effort to ascertain facts, in some ways impedes the learning process, in my opinion. In the meantime, I will continue to carry my children to the library and teach them the importance and process of performing research. And to ensure that my kids stay current, and when all else fails, I will simply hand them my phone or computer and encourage them to, "ask the smart Google lady."

Day 16 Laughter/Encouragement Capsule
"Vanity is the Last Thing to GO!"

I know plenty of women who traded in their cars for mini vans when they became mothers. Some did it with great elation and excitement, while others, with grave hesitation and trepidation. Me, I am not sure if it is vanity or the fact that I have sacrificed every mental, physical, emotional, social, financial, psychological, spiritual, and any other "al" ending word that incorporates my entire being, all for the sake of these kids.

I may be a 45-year-old stay home mom, but I like to think that I have swag, and am "PHAT" (pretty, hot and tempting). Grant it, I do not drive my dream car, which is an Exclusive Panamera Porsche, but in my brain damaged mommy mind, my Mercury Milan is just that. The children and I spend a large amount of time in my vehicle. It serves as a transportation service, office, bedroom, and kitchen to name a few.

So, let me ask you, in your office, bedroom and home, don't you decorate it in a way that reflects who you are? For me, the vehicle I drive must do that, especially since every other part of my life focuses on kids, hubby and our family. On a serious note, I do believe that some moms totally lose who they are; spirit, soul and body, once they become mothers, especially stay home moms.

It is very easy to get caught up in the daily routines of housework, homework, grocery shopping, carpooling, cooking, cleaning, extra curriculum activities, blah, blah, blah……. Then one day you wake up, look in the mirror and see a woman staring back at you that is unrecognizable. You have neglected your looks, weight, dreams, habits, hobbies, goals, sense of humor and even relationships, all for the betterment of the children.

Yes, your life must change some when you have children, but a woman should never forget that nurturing who she is, will in turn, make you a better nurturer for the children. I believe we moms can "have it all," just NOT at one time! The key is being patient and practical and never giving up on your dreams. Life is lived in seasons. A season to be young, middle aged, old. A season to be single, married, a parent of young kids, a parent of teens and a parent of adult children.

The way to prevent mommy depression is to know that no season last forever and that in each season, you MUST surround yourself with positive people, words, actions and mindsets. So, for me, choosing to not give into the "minivan mom" craze is something I chose to do to remind me that I am a woman / mom with swag and sex appeal.

If you drive a minivan because you love it, and/or it is practical, I am NOT telling you to trade in your vehicle for a convertible. Simply pinpoint at least one area that you have lost yourself in, and find yourself again. You rock, not because you are a mom, but because you are a female who is wonderfully made.

Day 17 Laughter Capsule
Put Your Distance Glasses On

You know you are getting older when your 4-year-old stands at your bedroom door holding a sign for you to read, and you, being only a few feet away can't make out the words, therefore causing your kid to yell, "Mom, put your distance glasses on!" Who would have thought that me, an almost 46-year-old woman would need "distance glasses" as my kid puts it? To add fuel to the fire, not only do I have "distance glasses" but about a year ago, I started wearing reading glasses. Where in the world did my perfect vision go?

I remember when I was a teen and young adult, I had 20/20 vision. I prided myself on having perfect vision during those years, especially since I struggled with an imperfect body and obesity. I would say to myself and others, "well, I may be overweight, but at least I can see like an eagle." Today my life has taken a 360-degree switch. I am no longer obese, but my eye sight is not as keen as it use to be. The reality is, I am not 20 years old anymore, and neither are my eyes. Instead of being devastated that my child is totally aware that I am getting older chronologically and visually, I chose to embrace it. I asked her to go into my purse, pull out my "distance glasses" and hand them to me.

Once I placed them on my aging eyes, I read a sign that brought a smile to my face and warmth to my heart. It simply read, "Mom, I love you!" Seeing that is worth any pair of eye glasses.

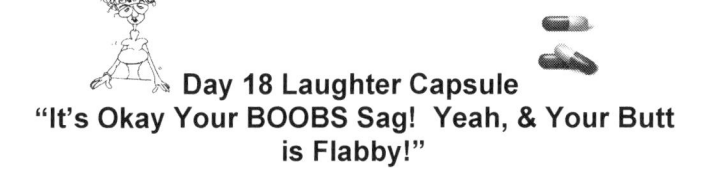

Day 18 Laughter Capsule
"It's Okay Your BOOBS Sag! Yeah, & Your Butt is Flabby!"

One drawback of allowing my daughters to hang out in our bedroom is the possibility that they may catch a glimpse of me running into the connected bathroom for a shower with just a bra and panty on. I try to be discreet with them seeing me less than dressed, however; since they are girls, I don't fret over an occasional bra and panty encounter, at least I didn't prior to their "eye opening" revelations about my boobs and rear end.

The other night, we had finished dinner, homework, and baths in record time. I told them they could watch Sponge Bob in our bedroom while I took a quick shower. I walked into the bathroom, turned on the shower and began to undress. As I overheard a barrage of laughter coming from the bedroom, I figured the girls were engrossed in their show, so I could run out, grab my night gown hanging on the closet door, all without them eyeing me.

I darted out the adjoined bathroom as if I were running the final leg of a race, landed in the room with just my bra and panties on, when suddenly I hear; "MOM, It's okay that your BOOBS sag!" At that moment, I was darn near deafened by the sound of uncontrollable, insane laughter. You would have thought my underwear wearing image was a new character on the Sponge Bob cartoon.

Next I hear, in a half intelligible voice, "Yeah, and your butt is flabby too!" Thankfully my self-esteem is not based upon my kid's opinions about my body. Yes, I know that my boobs do not sit up like a 23-year-old Swimsuit models. Neither does my butt look like the "after" photo in a Brazilian Butt Lift Plastic Surgeons office. But my God, do I cause them to crack up laughing like a cartoon?

The answer is NO, because after we all chuckled for a couple of minutes, the 8-year-old stated, "Mom, you are beautiful!" Then the 4-year-old adds; "Yeah, you are the best mommy EVER!" And I had to agree with them, saggy boobs, flabby butt and all.

Day 19 Laughter Capsule
The Back of my SUV Looked Like a Portable Day Care Center

When I became a new mom, to maintain some resemblance of mental stability, I made sure I was "pre-prepared!" Yes, you read it correctly, I said "Pre-prepared!" I was totally anxious and afraid that the kids would need something while we were away from home, and not have it.

So, I loaded up the back of my SUV as if it were a make shift day care center. You name it, I had it! Potty seat, blankets, extra set of clothes, wipes, water, pillows, jackets, snacks, portable DVD player, DVD's, toilet tissue, umbrellas, shoes, bleach (not sure why), and hand sanitizer.

For the life of my husband, he could not understand why I "NEEDED" all those items. Matter of fact, I can recall he and I engaging in some minor disagreements over, as he put it, "having all this junk in the vehicle!" One thing husbands need to realize, quick, fast and in a hurry, is that a mothers reasoning behind why we do what we do will seldom make sense to them. And I made sure, on numerous occasions, that when he would clean out my portable "day care" that he better NOT take a single item out!!!

Now that the children are older, I do not transport quite as many items as I use to. Another reason is because I am not as nervous and anxious as I use to be about being a mom. Have I totally overcome every mommy vice and worry? Of course not, and to prove it, I still keep two blankets, two small pillows, umbrellas, shoes, socks, potty seat, tissue, wipes and water in the trunk, just in case. Oh well, good habits die hard.

Day 20 Laughter Capsule
Did I Forget to Put Pants on This Morning?

Many new moms experience elation, as well as anxiety, thus leading to some behaviors that leave them, as well as others, scratching one's head. Anxiety is not funny, but one of the things that anxiety caused me to do is quite hilarious. Okay, here it goes..........

Whenever I would leave out the door, no matter the time of day, I would check to see if I had remembered to put pants or a skirt on the bottom half of my body! For some crazy reason, I mentally saw myself walking out the house without my bottom covered, only wearing my panties, showing everyone my tail! Had I ever walked out the door wearing only a shirt and panties? No, so I have no clue where this fear came from.

All I know, is for years, I would feel my legs and butt to ensure they were properly and modestly covered prior to walking out the front door. One gorgeous summer day, I woke and had the bright idea to walk baby Aunna to the mall. It would be an outing for her and a good workout for me. The sun was shining, and tons of my neighbors were outside washing their cars, grilling, playing cards, etc. You name it, people were taking advantage of the warm, yet non-humid weather we were experiencing.

Like any day, I carried out the stroller first, placed it on the front deck, then gathered Aunna and her baby bag, secured her in the stroller and walked to the edge of our drive way. The neighbors began their barrage of hellos and in an instant, the anxiety and fear kicked in. The moment I was fearing became a reality, almost.

I noticed that my legs felt the warm summer breeze, a feeling they normally never feel due to my preference for yoga or jogging pants. I feverishly began to pat my butt, legs, thighs, and hips as if I was putting out a fire, all while spinning in uncontrollable circles. OMG! By the time, I completed my last spin, my dear neighbor came running over to see if I had finally lost my mind.

"Angela, did a bug get on you? Why are you hitting yourself?" she asked. I frantically told her, I left out the house without any pants on, only wearing panties. This time she stared at me as if she was convinced I had lost my mind. She cautiously, and slowly guided my flailing hands to my thighs and instructed me to look down.

As I followed her directive, I realized that I was not showing my tail for the neighborhood to see, however, I did forget to change from my sleeping shorts. Phew! Thank God the neighbors only saw my legs and not my "onion." That day I learned a great lesson. Sleep only in yoga pants.

Day 21 Laughter Capsule
Thanks Lady for Making My Kids Cry, In the Store, at the Same Time

I am from the North and have lived in a few Northern states in my life, so I am use to people minding their own business and not wanting to get involved when and where it does not concern them. Some may call northerners rude, or uncaring, but that is not necessarily the case. It is simply the attitude of the culture. So, when we moved to the South a few years ago, it took me a while to get use to having complete strangers chime in and give their unsolicited opinions all willy-nilly.

My daughters and I could be at Walmart, Sears, Rite Aid, CVS, Kmart, restaurants, gas stations, anywhere, and like clockwork, someone who I have never met in my life would comment on something pertaining to my children. Two years ago, I was at Kmart picking up a few items for the house. Aunna was six and Lilly was two. At the time, Aunna sucked her thumb and Lilly sucked her two fingers, especially when they were sleepy. I was pushing Lilly in her stroller, Aunna was walking next to me, and both were sucking their respected fingers.

I knew it was nap time and the last place I should have been was out in a store, but I needed some laundry detergent and bleach. As I was rushing through the aisles to beat the "need a nap melt down" I heard a lady say, "Girl, your daughters are going to need braces if they don't stop sucking those fingers. I feel sorry for you!"

As if my two girls totally understood the full scope of what braces were, they both broke out into loud, uncontrollable sobs. These two children were crying buckets! I look over at the lady who was a STRANGER and said; "They will stop when they stop. I am not worried!"

I then turned and headed to the checkout counter. Unfortunately, the lines were too long and the volume and magnitude of my children's cries were a symphony of vocal crescendos. People were starting to stare and the last thing I needed was another COMPLETE STRANGER giving uninvited advice.

I put the items down on the nearest counter and left the store. Instead of leaving with laundry detergent and bleach, I left with two terrified, traumatized, sleepy, crying children. As I put them in their car seats, the six-year-old asked, with tears streaming down her cheeks, "mom, are we going to need braces like that lady said?" I said, "Honey, don't listen to that stupid woman. I use to suck my thumb when I was your age and I never wore braces. You and your sister will stop sucking your fingers very soon!"

She then asked, "Mom, is it okay if I suck my thumb now?" I told her to go right ahead and suck away. Before I could leave the Kmart parking lot, my two, gorgeous, finger sucking children were fast asleep and all I could do was take a deep breath and thank God above that I did not show that lady my two fingers!

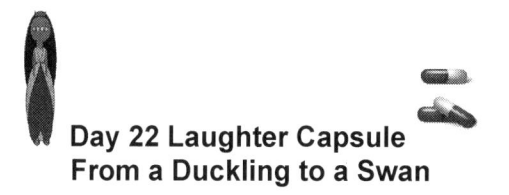

Day 22 Laughter Capsule
From a Duckling to a Swan

I pride myself on being a realist. Things are what they are. So, when our second daughter, Lilly was born, I was not delusional as to her appearance. She was not what some would call a "classic beauty." Lilly was very small, wrinkly and pale, but I did not care. In my eyes, she was perfect and pretty.

I remember being able to hold her in one hand and just rock her back and forth. I knew that some folks were saying she was "cute" just to be kind. I sincerely appreciated my dad's honesty a while ago, when he and my mom had come for a visit.

He walked into the house after a 4-hour car ride, hugged the girls and raved at how gorgeous they looked. He then hugged and kissed me, and said, "Angela, the girls look so happy and beautiful!" I thanked him and agreed. Then he followed with; "You know, when Lilly was a baby, I was so thankful she was healthy, because she was a tiny thing and very…." He stopped talking very abruptly, but knowing my dad's candor and honesty, I knew what he wanted to say, so I helped him finish his thought. I said, "Dad, I know, she was a bit funny looking when she was born!" We both laughed and then he whispered, "Yes, but look at her now, a true swan."

A lesson I always knew to be true has been affirmed by watching my Lilly go from a "baby duckling" to a gorgeous swan. Regardless of ones start in life, if you keep living, breathing and nurturing who you are, you will transform into something and someone quite breath taking. Today, my four-and-a-half-year-old girl is healthy, tall, smart and beautiful, inside and out. Now if only we can get her to stop wearing her favorite tutu seven days a week, 365 days a year, 24 hours a day!

Day 23 Laughter Capsule
Hey! You! The Loud Talking Bragging Mom, News Flash, Your Kid Sucks!

We have all been at kid events; whether it's soccer, ballet, football, band, karate, etc., and sitting behind you in the parent section is a loud talking mom who is raving about her kid's greatness like he/she is the second coming of Christ. And as you sit there, you glance at the mom and under your breath say, "Shut up, you liar." You know her kid is just like most of the other children there, flawed, yet talented, in their own right. And as she continues to gush about how polite, disciplined, neat, tidy, and cooperative her child is, you look over at her offspring and he/she is profusely digging in their nose, pulling out mucus and eating it as if it is Thanksgiving dinner.

The other day I was waiting for Aunna at ballet, sitting with the other parents, trying to take advantage of the only "kid free" hour I had, when big mouth "Lucy" is yucking it up bragging about her "brilliant, polite kid" and how she is above average in academics, sports, music and arts. Just the perfect child! As I kept glancing over at this woman, I noticed that most of the other parents were looking at her in disgust also. Not because we were jealous, but because for one, we were annoyed at the high-volume level she was dialoging in, and secondly, because we are realist and know that her child, like ours, are not "geniuses" in everything.

I am a great proponent for praising and being proud of my children, but also know that my kids do not and will not excel in everything. There will be subjects, activities and things that they will soar in, and other areas where they will totally suck at, and that is okay. That is what being human is all about. We do a disservice to our children when we constantly reward and praise them, even when they have failed or were defeated.

Also, children, like adults, are not pleasant all the time. They have good days as well as bad days. Some moments my children are as sweet and comforting as warm apple pie on a cold winters night. And other times, their actions resemble the Tasmanian devil himself.

As the hour was winding up, and my annoyance for this "proud" mom was wearing off, I began to feel sorry for her, especially after I, along with every parent there spotted her kid running out of ballet class yelling at the top of her lungs, "Mom, I want to eat at Burger King NOW, and you better not tell me NO!" That same, braggadocios mom turned three shade of red as she chuckled in embarrassment and gently said, "Katie, honey, you know I fix dinner every night and it is already prepared in the crock pot."

The icing on the cake, the cherry on top, the pièce de résistance that solidified for me that this kid was bad as hell, totally sucked and is stressing her mom out, was her daughter Katie's response; "Mom, stop lying, you don't know how to cook, grand mom does all the cooking!" You could hear a pin drop, and to be honest, I think I heard that poor mothers bottom lip hit the floor out of knowing that we all knew the truth.

So, in true Angela Johnson Ayers form, I tried to soften this ladies apparent and visible blow by saying, "Don't you just love crock pots? You can throw anything in them and voila, instant dinner." She gave me a timid, yet thankful grin, all while quickly gathering "bad behind" Katie's belongings and quietly left the building.

So, moms, what is the take away from this entry? Simply put, if you are an annoying bragging mom, be aware that kids, no matter how brilliant, are kids, and will embarrass you at the most inopportune times. And if you are ever around a loud talking, bragging parent, try to see through the smoke and mirrors and know that 9 out of 10 times, this mom is probably doing her best and needs some encouragement of her own. And if all else fails, sit somewhere else where the sound of her voice will not cause you to contemplate cutting off your ears.

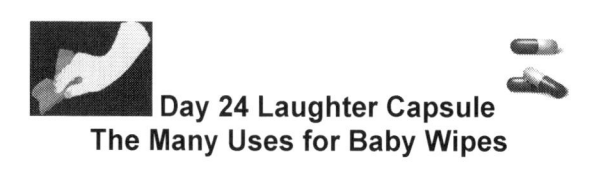

Day 24 Laughter Capsule
The Many Uses for Baby Wipes

Baby wipes are from Heaven! Prior to becoming a mother, I knew that baby wipes helped keep kids bottoms fresh and clean, but boy did I have an epiphany when I spilled coffee on the seats in my car. I was frantic, and as I searched for napkins in the glove compartment, all I had was the baby wipes stashed in the back. I grabbed a couple and as I commenced to wiping, I realized that not only were the coffee stains coming up, but so was a lot of God knows what.

After cleaning up all the coffee, I had a great idea. "If it cleans my seats so well, what else can these miracle baby wipes make spotless?" Before I knew it, I had wiped down the entire inside of the car. The dashboard, stirring wheel, seats, arm rest, even the windows. I darn near detailed the entire inside of the vehicle. I was on a cleaning frenzy. The lady parked next to me was staring at me as if I was wiping down a crime scene.

These astounding finds have made my husband a believer also, but it took the help of some "thick & spicy" steak sauce to validate that belief. For our Anniversary, Larry, the children and I went out to dinner. Amid his steak delight, he dropped a bunch of steak sauce on his shirt. Mind you, it did not stop him from eating, but it stopped me, because I knew I had a secret weapon in my purse. Before I could open my purse, our oldest daughter says, "mom is getting the baby wipes dad!" I did just that!

I began to wipe and wipe and wipe and before he could finish chewing his piece of steak, the huge stain was gone. Now, whenever we go out to eat, before we walk into the restaurant he asks, "Honey, do you have the baby wipes in your purse?" And you know I do.

One night I was laying in my bed and was too tired to get up and wash the makeup off my face. I was seriously contemplating sleeping with all the glop and goop on, but I dreaded staining my pillow case. I rolled over and to my surprise, I had a bag of baby wipes on my night stand.

I grabbed them as if my life depended on it and commenced to dabbing my face. Before I knew it, I had cleaned my entire face with these magical wipes. Let me just clarify that I am NOT a medical doctor, car detailing or baby wipe product expert. I am not suggesting you use these wipes on your car, clothes or face like I have done. I am simply sharing my experience and opinion. Now that being said, one of the million lessons I have learned while being a mother is when life gives you lemons, and you spill some of the lemon juice, clean up the mess with baby wipes (smile).

Day 25 Laughter Capsule
3pm Caffeine Injection

By 3 o'clock pm I am in desperate need of a major caffeine boost, and I know I am not alone. Whether you work outside the home or a stay at home mom, the need for this afternoon pick me up is real. By this time, the morning jolt has run out, the work day is not quite over, but you can see the light at the end of the tunnel. You are preparing for the commute home and/or to pick the kids up from school, take them to after school activities, meal preparation, homework help, clean up, baths, etc., etc., etc., et., ……. The list can go on and on, unlike your energy level.

The bottom line, most weekdays by this time, I am in desperate need of liquid caffeinated help. I know, I know, I know that some folks believe too much caffeine can have adverse effects on one's health. Since I am not a medical doctor, I am not suggesting you par take in my 3 pm coffee delight, however, if you have and choose to, just know I totally understand why.

Some of you may be Starbuck lovers like myself, but unfortunately, I do not have the money to support a daily habit of this, so I often opt for a simple cup of Joe from a less expensive place. But in a perfect world, I would have the financial means to afford a morning and afternoon Grande, soy, skinny vanilla latte with no foam courtesy of Starbucks. A girl can dream can't she.

While I am dreaming, wouldn't it be grand if I had the money to hire a nanny, housekeeper and driver to tend to the kids, clean the house and transport me to get my morning and afternoon latte? Or better yet, have the money to have a personal Starbucks barista assigned to me and bring me a latte on demand? Oh yeah, that is the life.

Well, back to reality. Fellow moms, I use to feel like such a "mommy failure" over my need for an afternoon pick me up. I mean really, shouldn't I have enough energy from my morning workout to tie me over all day? But the truth is, I do not. When I meet other moms who are in the same boat, I don't feel as bad.

I have now let go of the guilt and embraced the sisterhood that I am a part of. To psychologically feel better about my indulgence, I no longer drink a huge, gravy bowl size cup of joe, instead I have a very petit, tea cup size one. Hopefully, very soon, I will not need this afternoon jolt at all, but until my change comes, a mom got to do, what a mom got to do!

Day 26 Laughter Capsule
"I am a Real Housewife"

Moms, I have a guilty pleasure and I am mature enough to admit it. I watch the Real Housewives franchise that comes on Bravo television. I am sure many of you do too, but my reason for doing so may differ from yours. My hubby thinks I watch it because I love the bickering and cattiness, but the truth is, I view it because I am amazed that grown women, who are mostly moms, have the time and energy to bicker, fuss and fight.

I also view to see how lavish their lives are and transcend my mind to how totally different from some of them I would be if I had their cash. They are so fortunate to afford help to alleviate the physical demands of being a wife and mother. Think about how relaxed and well rested you would be if you had live in nannies, cooks, maids, and drivers?

It appears these ladies have it all, but they still find time and strength to bicker and plot on one another. I know a lot of it is for the show since drama is what draws ratings, but my goodness. If they had to live in my reality for a week, some of them would jump off the nearest curve and run to the hills in their heels.

You may be wondering how I have the time to watch these shows due to the demands of being a mom and wife. Thank goodness for on Demand and being able to record, pause, rewind and fast forward shows. Sometimes it takes me two days to watch one program, but I get through it. Usually I am folding or ironing clothes while watching these shows and shaking my head all at the same time, in a state of disbelief.

How do they find the strength to argue and scheme after doing their "housewife" responsibilities? By the end of my busy days of taking care of kids, and all that it includes, I have no energy for much of nothing. Being a housewife is constant work, from sun up to sun down and all through the night.

I wish I had the money to create my own show that would follow ordinary moms/housewives around with cameras capturing what really takes place. I would name the show, "A FOR REAL Housewife of…..." I fear that people who watch the housewife shows of today are getting the wrong perception of what our jobs entail. It is not all glamorous clothes, fancy cars, nannies, afternoon lunches with champagne and trips to Greece.

I have come up with other names for a real-life housewife show that encompasses all things housewife. Here are a few of them:

1. *The Low Down Dirty Truth Housewife Show*
2. *The, Are You Sure You Want to Be a Housewife Show?*
3. *Cooking, Cleaning, Ironing and Mending Housewife Show*
4. *The Shut Up Back There, Stop Hitting Your Brother, Clean Your Room Housewife Show.*
5. *Diary of an Insane Housewife*
6. *The Many Faces on Housewife Lane*
7. *The I Went to College for This Housewife Show*
8. *Only the Strong Will Survive Housewife Show*

Although my daily life is not chronicled on TV for the world to see, those most near and dear to me see and appreciate what I do, and those people are my hubby and children. Would I love to have the money like some of these ladies? Of course! Would I give my left toe to reside in a mansion with live in nannies, cooks, maids and drivers? You bet your bottom dollar!

Since that is not the case, I will simply be thankful for what I do have and relish in the fact that when I do have the time to visit with friends, we have productive, life giving conversations instead of arguing and plotting. And if I ever get the chance to create a show, stay tuned, you may be contacted to appear (smile).

Day 27 Laughter Capsule
Coffee Creamer in the Kids Orange Juice

When I wake in the morning, I know that once the girls roll out of bed, it is on like popcorn. Children have endless energy, and they do not care if you had a horrible night sleep, or your mind has been bombarded with worries due to bills, health, etc. When children wake in the mornings all they care about are two things; 1. What they are going to eat and 2. What fun things are they going to do. And in that order.

So, one summer morning, like clockwork, they woke at 7:00 am. I heard them make their beds, gather their night time water bottles and walk down the stairs. They sashayed into our bedroom, without an invitation mind you, and announced, "We're up!" They proceeded to the family room where the oldest turns on the television and commenced to filling their minds with Sponge Bob.

After 7-10 minutes I hear, "mom, we're hungry!" Then, I yell back, "What do you want to eat?" The 4-year-old utters, "I want to go to IHOP for breakfast!" I assure her that her request will not be filled and to rethink her breakfast choice. Mind you, we do love IHOP, however, eating there every day as she requests daily, is not a viable option.

Anyway, they usually settle for cereal, or toast with eggs, or sausage, or biscuits, or pancakes, or waffles. So, this morning, I go to the kitchen and begin preparing eggs and toast. While spreading butter on their toast, the 8-year-old yells, "Mom, don't forget the orange juice please." Like any good mom, I take out the OJ from the refrigerator, pull out their cups and begin to pour their juice, all while thinking, "boy I NEED some coffee N O W!!!!"

I walk over to the Keurig, turn it on and pray that it will somehow, supernaturally dispense my coffee as soon as I push the power button. It does not, so as I waited, I forgot that I had already poured their juice into their cups, however, I did remember that I needed cream in my coffee, French vanilla crème that is. So, I take the creamer out the frig and hear a barrage of, "mom, we are thirsty, did you forget about our orange juice?"

I commence to "pour" their juice when I notice that the juice was white! OMG!

Not only had I already poured juice in their cups, but now I was adding my creamer to it! "I used to be a brilliant woman before having these kids," is the first thought that came to mind. "Oh well," I think, "they say certain vitamins are available that can enhance brain clarity and memory, but until I buy some, this coffee must do!" I quickly took the kids their breakfast and juice and then savored every drop of my coffee.

Day 28 Encouragement Capsule
"Getting A Break From It All"

I have been a biological mom for 8 years, and not until a year ago, did I realize the mental, physical, and emotional importance of getting some alone time. I thought the hour and a half I worked out at the gym while Lilly was at the gyms day care, and Aunna was in school was enough "me" time. That was not the case. Although I have no kids around me while exercising, Lilly is still there and my mind is occupied with rushing to finish before her lunch and nap time.

My days were all the same; take care of kids, cook, clean, iron, bills, grocery shop, juggle finances, set up and take them to doctor appointments, etc., etc., all while trying to nurture my creative and productive side with little to no success. And let's not talk about not having an ounce of desire or patience for my husband. I was drained.

Year after year, month after month, day after day, I found myself not sleeping, irritable, exhausted, depressed and sad. I began to resent being a wife, mother and stay home mom. On top of all that, feelings of guilt and self-condemnation flooded my heart and mind for having these thoughts in the first place. I kept asking myself, "Angela, why aren't you happy? You always wanted a loving husband and great, healthy kids. You have it and you are still unhappy."

I felt like a failure and ungrateful to God, when I was very grateful, but the feelings of despair and depression seemed so powerful. The final straw came one evening when I just snapped. I began yelling, crying and screaming uncontrollably. I was inconsolable.

Larry took the kids upstairs to bed, and thankfully they fell fast asleep. When he came back to our room, I was still sobbing. After about an hour of my emotions flooding out, Larry and I talked for three more hours. I shared everything I had inside, the good, bad and ugly truths. That night when I feel asleep, I slept like a baby, something I hadn't done in years, literally.

I felt better for a few weeks, then BAM, another crying, screaming, anxiety filled outbreak. After this one, I knew I needed some professional help. After speaking with a Counselor/Psychologist, and my husband, I realized that I was suffering from anxiety, and depression, and one of the triggers came from not taking time for myself. I was also doing too much in a single day.

Taking time for oneself does not mean having to vacate at the spa for four hours a day. Sounds nice, but I don't have that much time or money. Getting time for self can be as simple as going for a 30-minute drive alone or taking a long walk. The point is doing absolutely nothing related to kids and hubby.

I've also learned to listen to my emotions, body and mind as to when I am in desperate need of a break. When I find myself feeling irritated, and snapping at simple questions the family may ask of me, I know I need to slow down and step back. Just the other weekend I saw the signs, so I grabbed my blanket and pillow and told Larry that I was going upstairs to be alone and not to let the kids disturb me. I slept for 4 hours.

Ladies, you must listen to your mind and body and give it what it needs so you can be mentally, emotionally and psychologically healthy. I no longer feel guilty for needing a break. I use to see it as a sign of weakness when hearing other moms speak about requiring a break from it all. "How weak and pitiful are these women," is what I would say under my breath. Now I know that it is wise and detrimental, and has nothing to do with weakness. Real strength is knowing your limitations and seeking help in whatever fashion that's appropriate for you.

I have also surrendered to the idea of being "imperfect!" I thought if I completed all my household chores in one day, that somehow, I was an outstanding and flawless mom. But the reality is, I am outstanding when I am mentally healthy and joyful, not sad, angry and depressed. Would my kids rather have a perfectly clean house with a stressed-out mom, or a moderately clean and tidy home with a loving mother. The answer is the latter.

So moms, if you are struggling with any of these warning signs of sadness, anxiety, depression, anger, etc., please, please, please seek some professional help. There is no shame in that at all. Secondly, take some time daily for just yourself, even if it's a 10-minute stroll with just you and your thoughts.

Third, try not to pack on too much into one day. Spread out your weekly task so you don't find yourself working from sun up to sun down, and lastly, fill your mind with positive, self-esteem building thoughts. All I use to see were my mistakes and shortcomings as a mother, now, I see them, but I don't dwell on it.

On a lighter note, I am not giving you carte blanche to allow your home to become a pigsty either. Maintaining some order and neatness aids in improving your mindset and attitude. A cluttered home, a cluttered mind. Balance is key and I have a feeling you and I are going to be just fine!

Day 29 Encouragement Capsule
SEX? Now? Are You For REAL?

My husband could be sick, dying and one foot in the grave and he would still muster up enough strength to want to "boom shock, shock, BOOM," if you get my drift. A very big disagreement erupted between my husband and I surrounding one word, SEX, and his timing for wanting it. Let me tell you how it all went down…….

It was almost two years ago, and I was physically, emotionally, and mentally exhausted. I was exercising vigorously almost every morning, but not feeding my body enough fuel to carry out my daily task. I was anemic, my white blood count was dangerously low and I was taking in entirely too much coffee. I convinced myself that I needed three to four 16 oz. cups of caffeine to keep up with my daily demands, but it was beyond that.

The main reason for my exhaustion and mood swings was, I was pushing myself too hard. From 6:45 am when the kids woke, to 8:00 pm when they went to bed, I was going at full speed ahead. Some days I would literally only sit down while the girls ate their lunch and dinner. In between I was up on my feet cleaning, cooking, laundry, running errands, grocery shopping, etc., etc., etc. And to top it all off, due to all the caffeine, I was not sleeping well at night.

I was also very stressed out about Aunna starting school, finding the right school for her, our finances, personal health issues, our son, life worries, etc., etc. I also wasn't taking any time for myself. I was simply EXHAUSTED! A recipe for disaster.

It was 8:45 pm and I was DONE, you hear me, DONE! I had a trying long day with the kids and had fought a long, hard 45-minute battle of "get your butt in the bed and stay in the bed!" I had finally won the battle, could hear the children snoring, so I rushed into the kitchen, poured myself a "respectable" size glass of wine and walked into our bedroom, sat on the bed and sighed.

I took one sip of wine, turned on the television, and for a moment, I felt as if my life had transcended back to my days as a single woman, when I did not have to answer to or be responsible for anyone but myself. Oh, what a great feeling. I was alone! Kids were in rooms sleep, hubby was in our family room watching a random "kill-em-up" movie, and all was silent......for literally two minutes. THEN, Larry walks in, sits down in his chair next to his side of the bed and ask; "So, are you ready to have sex yet?"

WHATTTTTTTT! I was furious, but I also felt hurt. I told him OFF, and I meant every word. All day I had and always am catering to someone's needs and wants, and for the first time all day, I had just sat down to cater to myself, and then here he comes, another person wanting what they want from poor, exhausted me. I took it personally.

While I was fussing, and cussing at him, I was also crying, because I literally felt like everyone around me only used me for what they wanted, starting with the kids and ending with him. I also reminded him that while he was away from home working, lunching, and communicating with other adults and nurturing his creative side, I was here, ALONE with his children making his house and theirs a happy, high functioning home.

Furthermore, I felt the need to refresh his memory that every evening, I make sure the girls and I give him time to "unwind" from work before we bombard him. This particular evening, he had gotten home, went to his desk to handle some work calls. After talking on the phone for about an hour, he fixed his plate and went into the family room to eat his dinner, all while I was doing homework with the girls, bathing the kids, etc.…

So, when he approached me for sex that night, all my feelings came crashing down and I felt everyone around me wanting what they wanted and draining me emotionally, physically, mentally and in regards to him, sexually. The truth is, I am very thankful that my husband desires me and still finds me attractive and alluring, but in that moment, I just wanted no one wanting anything from me.

Today, two years later, Larry has been well trained (smile)! He knows to give me some much-needed down time after we put the children to bed. He doesn't ask me any questions during that time. Matter of fact, he usually goes into a totally different room so I can have some time alone.

Although I hate how heated our argument got that one fateful night, I am thankful for the outcome. At the time, I wish I could have expressed my exhaustion and stress prior to the argument, but I honestly did not know just how wore out I was, not until my cup had "runneth over."

So, women, if your man seems to have a one-track mind pertaining to sex, do not do like I did and call him everything but a child of God. Instead, sit down calmly when the children are not around and tell him how you feel. Try to come up with a compromise. And when all else fails, on those nights where you can't muster up an ounce of strength to give some "sexual healing," get in the bed and snore like a cave man! Just don't do this too often!

Day 30 Encouragement Capsule
"The <u>**KNOW IT ALL FRIEND**</u> from HELL!"

Have you ever heard these words from a friend; "Girl, if those were my children I would ...." Or, "What you need to do is..............." I have gotten these unsolicited gems from one or two people, who funny enough, DO NOT even have children. Now please don't misunderstand, I do believe that God has given great wisdom to some females who have a mother's heart, although they may not have birthed a child of their own. But those are not the people I am referring to.

I am talking about those "know it all," "get on your last nerve," "wish they would shut the heck up" people, who think they know everything there is to know about being a mother and "think" they hold all of life's child rearing truths. I call them the "Want to be Miyagis" of mommy hood! They are wannabe experts in the areas of discipline, bed time routines, how a child should eat, talk, learn, potty train, and all things children.

Most often, these people are either extremely hard-nosed, beat your child authoritarians or ridiculously laid back and anything goes specialist. Prior to marriage and mommy hood, I worked for years in the education field. I must admit, I was one of those "know it all's" who had an answer for every parent and/or friend that inquired and those that did not. Years later, when I finally became a mother, I had to apologize to one of my dearest friends, Judy.

She had children years before I did. She would call me and be venting about her children, and instead of quietly listening and being a sounding board, I would offer unsolicited input. I know I got on her nerves, but she was too gracious and loving of a person to say so.

You see, it is very easy to give logical, text book advice to a parent, but parenting is not simply logical or practical. Being a parent is emotional first. Once one becomes a mom, your heart burst open and exposes you to a love, and passion that only parenthood can create.

Most people who have not experienced this occurrence personally, will often offer advice that lacks the emotional component. When I miscarried a child in 2010, those who knew offered their sympathy and concern, however; the greatest comfort I received came from those who personally endured this same traumatic event. They had empathy instead of just sympathy. Per Google.com, "sympathy is defined as feelings of pity and sorrow for someone else's misfortune, where empathy is the ability to understand and share the feelings of another."

The same is true for issues pertaining to mommy hood and parenting. Therefore, if you are asking yourself how you should handle a "know it all, know nothing friend," I suggest the following:

- Determine if their critiques are coming from a loving place, or a critical one.
- If it is from a loving place, eat the meat of their statements and spit out the bones.
- If the advice is harsh, critical, judgmental and could come from a root of jealousy, you may want to sever the relationship all together.
- If you sense the relationship is worth saving, have a conversation explaining how it makes you feel when she offers unsolicited input. Come to an agreement that advice on parenting is welcome only when it's invited.

Parenting is not a science and neither are friendships, but once you get to the root of the issues, there is always a solution.

Day 31 Encouragement Capsule
Living Out This Season of Your Life with Joy

Well moms, I hope this 31-day supply of laughs mixed with a few serious entries has brought you some much needed joy and a sense that you are not alone on this child-rearing journey. Every night when I lay down, I must remind myself that I am not perfect, neither am I a perfect mom. I make mistakes and each day must ask God to give me wisdom, knowledge and understanding on how to raise these gifts he entrusted me with.

At times, I feel extremely overwhelmed, but it's in those moments that I must pull on the strength of my husband, God and other family and true friends. If you are married, please try to not forget to nurture your relationship with your spouse. Often, I give so much to the children, till I forget or neglect to give to the one who helped make these children possible, my Larry.

When I became a mom, my entire focus was on nurturing and caring for the children, but I realize that one day these children will be adults and on their own. Then it will be Larry and I again, and I don't want to be sitting across from a stranger because we forgot to nurture one another during our kid's younger years. So, moms, spend quality time with your mates.

And for you single moms, please know that I recognize all the hard work you put in daily. I commend and encourage you to keep on being a shining example to your children of what perseverance looks like. As mothers, whether married or single, it is so easy to get bogged down with the minutia of life and simply surviving, till we forget to seize the moment.

Our children are truly a gift, even those times they are arguing and acting a fool! I use to find myself wishing that they would hurry up and grow up so I could "get Angela back!" But the reality is, when I rush this journey, I miss out on all the lessons and blessings God has for me. So, let's enjoy mommy hood one day at a time and keep a joyful attitude in the process.

Much love and laughter,

Angela Johnson Ayers

About the Author

"I find life so interesting and the people in it even more fascinating! We have many differences and even greater similarities. My life purpose is to create platforms of dialogue to encourage, enlighten, and challenge people in every area of their lives. I am in my element when I am using my voice facilitating workshops, speeches, and lectures on such topics as motherhood, weight/obesity, anxiety, self-esteem, emotional abuse, and relationships to name a few. I was blessed with the gift of gab, and I love using it to empower others!" *Angela Johnson Ayers*

Angela Johnson Ayers, a Maryland native is the second oldest of six children. She has two loving parents who have been married for over 50 years. Angela obtained a Master degree in Public Administration in 1996 and a Bachelor's in Political Science in 1993. Her vast knowledge, skills and abilities allowed her to acquire occupations in the areas of education, politics and the nonprofit sector. She has worked as a Middle School Principal, Educational Consultant, Political Consultant and Program Manager, to name a few.

In 1998 Angela became a published author of the book, "***Helpful Hints for College Bound Students,***" a book that covers every aspect of college; from packing, to choosing a major. Penn State University, Hoop Dreams Inc., The Congressional Youth Leadership Council, along with various churches and educational groups invited Angela to present on the books topics. "Although I have held diverse and interesting jobs, my true love and passion has always been to help others overcome and soar."

Mrs. Johnson-Ayers desire to help others reach their personal, social, relational, emotional, physical and professional goals was birthed through much pain, negative self-talk and low self-esteem. "I know what it's like to feel invisible. To be put down, teased and mistreated simply because you do not fit the status quo. During most of my life, I was very overweight. My struggle with weight impacted me tremendously.

I felt like I was less due to my size. I allowed my obesity to place me in a downward spiral of bad relationships and self-sabotaging actions and situations." Throughout much of Angela's' teen and adult life, she would lose 100 lbs. only to gain it back again, over and over and over. In 2006, Angela tipped the scales at her heaviest weight of 318 lbs. Today she has lost over 140 lbs.

In 2007 Angela became a certified fitness instructor and certified personal trainer. As she explains in her wellness workshops, anyone who needs to get healthy must find the path that works for them. "Bariatric surgery helped put me on a path to better health. It is not for everyone, and no matter what weight loss path one takes, the transformation must start from the inside /out." Angela now uses all she learned through her weight struggles, battle with low self-esteem, and many of life's trials, and created *"Enhancing Beauty from the Inside/Out"* workshops.

These workshops aid women of all ages, cultures and walks of life in identifying emotional, relational, mental, and physical barriers to positive self- esteem, positive image, career achievement, relational success and overall life satisfaction. She also provides fashion advice for all body types, make-up techniques, skin and hair care strategies and exercise pointers for all weight categories.

Angela pursued a career in modeling and was a contestant in the 2000 Ms. plus USA Pageant.

Angela's second love is being on stage. "I have been acting, dancing and performing ever since I was 5 years old. I danced for RJV Dance Company from ages 5-17.
 As a young girl, my dad got us a huge podium and had us consistently practice using proper diction, elocution, and articulation by memorizing and/or reciting poems, plays, speeches, etc. I must admit, I LOVE the stage and in my most un-humble voice, it loves me back!"

Angela is also the writer, producer and actor of **"Well I'll be Darn, I'm Okay After All."** A one woman play that takes the audience through a visual, mental and emotional journey through Angela's life dealing with love, loss, weight, body image, a verbally abusive first marriage and the road back to redemption. The play debuted in 2008 in Philadelphia, PA and received rave reviews.

In 2008, Angela gave birth to she and husband Larry's their first child together. Angela endured many of the ups and downs that come with being a new mother. "The second I delivered Aunna, I literally felt fear enter my heart, mind and emotions. I experienced postpartum depression like so many women do. In 2012, after giving birth to our second daughter Lillian, I felt like I had a slightly better handle on mommy hood. During my journey of being a new mom, and a stay home mom at that, I battled feelings of depression, guilt, professional stagnation, burn out, and personal unfulfillment." After conversing with other moms, Angela realized that a large majority shared her same emotions.

So, in 2013, Angela, along with renowned author Tracey Michae'l Lewis-Giggetts co-wrote the Kindle eBook, ***"Blast Off! Launching You into Motherhood- A 21 Day Devotional for the New Mom."*** This short daily devotional gives new and seasoned moms a chance to steal a few precious moments to refuel and regain a clearer perspective into being mom. It can be purchased on amazon.com

In 2014 Angela launched her YouTube channel, Life ***Can Not Weight***. It provides insightful and entertaining short videos for anyone desiring to lose and/or maintain weight loss. In 2013, Angela became a "mommy blogger" and created www.confessionsofmommie.blogspot.com Angela and Larry reside in North Carolina and are enjoying raising their two daughters. To contact Angela

for speaking engagements or questions, email her at
abjconsultingllc@gmail.com

Connect With Angela Johnson Ayers

I really appreciate you reading my book! Here are my social media coordinates:

Website: https://www.angelajohnsonayers.com

Blogsite: https://confessionsofmommie.blogspot.com/

Twitter: @laughterformoms

Email me: abjconsultingllc@gmail.com

CreateSpace: https://www.createspace.com/6958505

Podcast: https://www.spreaker.com/user/lifecannotweight

YouTube:https://www.youtube.com/channel/UCv4eq2B5av6l_R_QwwhzaiQ

End Notes

Google.com 2017

Clipart images: https://openclipart.org

Made in the USA
Columbia, SC
03 January 2022